Ginger England Burrows

Oscar and His Magical Tree

This book is dedicated to:
My late beautiful sister Marcy <u>Faye</u>
England, and to my late dear friend
Hugh Harris; the voice of NASA.
Thank you both for believing in me.

Chapter 1

A Very Small Troll in Norway

Once upon a time, there was a troll who lived in a tree. This was not just any ole troll and it was not just any ole tree; this troll and this tree were very special!

The troll's name was Oscar. Oscar was a very small troll and was beautiful! Oscar had a cute little nose, and big, beautiful, green eyes. His feet and hands were excessively big for his body, and his hair was bright golden yellow full of curls that felt and looked like silk. He had six toes on each foot, and three fingers and a thumb on each hand, and he stood one foot and two inches tall. He was not like most trolls; he was small and sweet!

Oscar was born a very long time ago in Tønsberg, Norway. Most of the trolls in

Norway were big, ugly, and mean but Oscar was just the opposite. He came from a family of small trolls, but Oscar was still especially small even though he had come of age. His parents felt that if the large local trolls saw Oscar, they would harm him, so they kissed him goodbye and put him on a ship that set sail to England where they knew no other trolls lived.

Oscar was afraid and did not want to leave his parents. His parents were sad but knew they were doing the right thing by sending him away to keep him safe from harm. Before Oscar left, his father Clarence gave him a magical seed. He told Oscar to take the seed and plant it when he gets where he is going and after a few days, a big tree will grow that will be his home. He told him that the tree would not be an ordinary tree. He said that the tree will be invisible to all others except him, and because the tree is magical, he will be

able to travel anywhere in the world that he wishes to go, and back, including his home in Norway. He said the tree would also produce whatever food he wished so he would never go hungry. He also warned Oscar to tell no one about his magical tree! This assured Oscar that he would indeed be safe and would still be able to visit his family whenever he wanted to. So, Oscar took his magical seed, placed it in his pocket, climbed aboard the ship, and off he went!

Chapter 2

Oscar Begins His Journey

After a whole week of being tossed about back and forth by the waves of the ocean and being cramped up in a crate where he hid from the crew, the ship finally docked just before nightfall. Oscar got up and stretched his arms, took a deep breath, and climbed off the ship to see the new land. There were a lot of people meeting the ship so Oscar ran little by little, hiding behind luggage, crates, garbage cans, and whatever else he could find to conceal himself until he finally made it up the dock and into the forest.

In the forest, the first thing he stumbled upon were bushes that had fresh berries, and he was very hungry, so he picked lots of the berries and used his shirt to hold them. He then found a big tree with a lot of leafy limbs that looked like a good place to rest, so he ran up the tree and snuggled in for the night. Just as he was dozing off, he felt and heard the ground shaking, so he peeked out of the leaves, and he saw a huge goblin sniffing in the air. "Oh no," he thought, "Is this creature smelling me"? Just as those words crossed his mind, the goblin walked right up to Oscar still sniffing. "You smell delicious darling" she said to Oscar in a very divine voice. "Please don't eat me" says Oscar, "I'm not that kind of girl darling, I like blueberries and strawberries darling" she said. "What is your name"? He replied "Oscar," she said, "and I am Elle, it is very nice to meet you darling"! As he got a better look at Elle, he noticed that she was wearing a whimsical dress that was long and had pretty colors of pink, yellow, orange, and green on it. She was also bald headed, barefoot with exceptionally large feet, had big lips, big pointy ears, and wore bright pink lipstick; she was very lady like!

Oscar offered her some of the berries that he picked, and she gladly accepted. She said, "this looks like a good place to rest for the evening darling, if you don't mind," so she lay at the foot of the tree, and they slept through the night, both snoring, comfortably!

The next morning, as the sun was rising, Oscar woke to the sounds of birds singing. He woke up well rested and yawned and stretched and then suddenly remembered that he had met a friend, or he thought in a half-awakened slumber, maybe he had just dreamed it! Then suddenly, he heard a loud snore and looked down and there she was, still sleeping at the foot of the tree. With a snarky smile, he broke off some twigs and dropped them one by one on her head and she jerked each time one hit her, and then she finally woke up. She looked up, saw Oscar, and said while batting her eyes, "Well good morning darling, did you sleep well"?

He replied, "Yes I did, thank you." She said, "Let's get some breakfast, and then I shall show you around the forest," he thought that was a wonderful idea, so they got up, picked fresh berries, and found a stream to sit by and enjoyed their breakfast talking to one another.

During their conversation, Oscar asked Elle where he was exactly, and she explained to him that he was in an area called Newcastle, and that she had lived there in those woods her whole life. She said that there are others like her, but they were not quite as nice, and he told her about his family back in Norway and why he was sent away.

After breakfast and their conversation, Elle walked Oscar around the forest resting him on her shoulder. She showed him a beautiful area that was lush green and full of blooming flowers, had a crystal-clear mountain stream running through it, and had lots of big trees.

She told him that it was her favorite place, and that no one ever came to this area, so she loved to come here for the quiet and peacefulness that it gave; she called it the Flowery Forest. Oscar thought to himself that this would be the perfect spot to plant his seed!

As the day grew long, Elle told Oscar that she had to go home but that she would be back in the morning. Oscar and Elle said their goodbyes and Elle went home. Oscar was left in the Flowery Forest alone and thought it would be the perfect time to find a spot for his tree. He walked along the edge of the stream and found a beautiful spot full of lovely flowers that was a bit away from the beaten path, so he dug a deep hole, and planted the seed that his father had given him. He then laid up against a tree close to his planted seed, covered himself up with leaves that he found, and fell asleep.

Early the next morning, he woke up to the sound of breaking twigs and rustling leaves and was startled. He slowly peeked his eyes over the shrubs to look and see who was making the noise and was at ease when he realized that it was just a family of deer passing through. Oscar wiped his brow in relief, and as his hand passed over his eyes, he saw something on his left thumb that he had never seen before; there was a shiny silver ring there that had many little, tiny silver leaves on it! This must have something to do with the tree he thought; he tried to take it off to look at it closer, but it would not budge! He dozed back off for a few hours after admiring the ring and finally was woken by the beautiful sound of singing birds, the trickling of the water running down stream, and the smell of lemony crumpets!

He sniffed in the air as the smell grew stronger and then he heard and felt the ground shake. "Oscar darling where are you?" yelled Elle. He then ran closer because he did not want Elle, or anyone knowing the area of his tree, and met her in the middle of a small pasture full of flowers. As they saw one another, Oscar yelled and waved as he closely approached her "Top of the morning to you my dear Elle", and they both sat down on a soft blanket that she brought, ate the warm, soft, delicious crumpets smothered in warm vanilla icing with the creamiest butter he had ever had, and drank hot tea with honey and fresh cream; Elle was proving to be a wonderful friend for he couldn't have dreamed of having such a wonderful breakfast in the middle of a strange forest!

Chapter 3

Elle Shows Oscar His New Land

During breakfast, Elle told Oscar that there was a small town that sat just over two mountains away from them, and that she wanted to take him and show him the town and said that they could make a day of it. Oscar thought that was a wonderful idea, so they got up and off they went! Oscar, of course, sat on Elle's shoulder for the trip because her stride was much larger and faster than his.

It took them half a day to make the trip and once they arrived, they thought they had better just sit outside the town and wait for nightfall to come to go in. They could not let people see them because people feared creatures of their kind. When nightfall came, they began to see lights go out in the town one by one;

people were turning in for bed and that was just the sign they had been waiting for.

Up, and into the town they went! Elle was particularly good at hiding because she had been doing it her whole life; she knew how to tip-toe and how to stay in the shadows. Elle tip-toed all through the town jumping quietly from shadow to shadow as she and Oscar looked through the store windows and smelled the fresh pies and breads baking for the next day. As they stood in the shadows, they listened to the stories that people told about their day, and they saw ladies squeezing fresh snonkelberries for juice and watched them fill up barrels and place them outside the stores. They got very hungry after watching and smelling all the delightful scents, so Elle decided that she must get them some of them delicious treats to take back with them.

She could not just walk up and buy the items from the town folk because seeing her would terrify them and she knew it. So, she decided to leave money in place of the items she took; she was a lady, not a thief! She needed something to put the wonderful food in and saw a sack full of potatoes lying by a door, so she grabbed the sack and dumped out the potatoes. She and Oscar then hopped through the shadows buying pies, bread and fruit until the potato sack was full and then headed back out of town. Just before they ran out of the town gate, she saw a big barrel of snonkelberry juice and grabbed it too. They then slipped out of town with lots of goodies and not one person saw them; the day was a success!

As Oscar and Elle headed back to their forest, they realized how tired they were, and both thought that it would be a good idea to rest and finish the trip in the morning;

BAKERY

so, they found a cozy cave and built a small fire. They pulled out two savory meat pies, two loaves of bread, some fruit, and then had a feast! Oscar was very thirsty after his meal and asked Elle for some of the snonkelberry juice. He told her that he had never heard of a snonkelberry before and asked her what it was. Elle told Oscar that snonkelberry juice is something she grew up drinking and that snonkelberries can only be found in the mountains in Northern England. She told him that it was expensive and that people from around the world go there just to get the juice. She described the berry as being big, round, purple, green, and sweet. She said that the juice, when poured, comes out with a purple color on the bottom, and a green color on the top. Oscar could not wait to try this amazing juice, so he had Elle pick up the barrel and pour some into his mouth. As he drank the juice, his skin began turning purple and he

so, they found a cozy cave and built a small fire. They pulled out two savory meat pies, two loaves of bread, some fruit, and then had a feast! Oscar was very thirsty after his meal and asked Elle for some of the snonkelberry juice. He told her that he had never heard of a snonkelberry before and asked her what it was. Elle told Oscar that snonkelberry juice is something she grew up drinking and that snonkelberries can only be found in the mountains in Northern England. She told him that it was expensive and that people from around the world go there just to get the juice. She described the berry as being big, round, purple, green, and sweet. She said that the juice, when poured, comes out with a purple color on the bottom, and a green color on the top. Oscar could not wait to try this amazing juice, so he had Elle pick up the barrel and pour some into his mouth. As he drank the juice, his skin began turning purple and he

started bouncing on his bottom around in a circle. He felt so happy, and the juice was so delicious he began laughing uncontrollably. As soon as the bouncing stopped, he let out a loud burp and his purple skin faded; Elle laughed so hard at him and told him that when he got used to drinking the juice, he would not bounce and turn purple anymore. They then both laid down and got comfortable for the night, watching the fire burn out as they finally dozed off.

The next morning Oscar woke up, and the first thing that he noticed was the ring on his thumb, it had changed overnight; the ring was now covered in tiny green leaves. This was very interesting to him, and he knew that something had to have happened to the tree while he was gone, so he eagerly shook and awoke Elle so they could get back to their Flowery Forest.

Chapter 4

Oscar Meets His Magical Tree

Oscar and Elle approached their forest just before nightfall, and Oscar could see a big colorful tree peeking out above all the other trees in the distance; he knew that it must be his tree, and he was extremely excited. Elle took Oscar back to the Flowery Forest and told him that she needed to go home, and that she would see him the next day. As she departed, Oscar ran quickly to where he had planted his seed, and when he reached the spot, he was in awe of what he saw. It was the most beautiful tree he had ever laid his eyes on. It was very tall and very wide, was full of colorful leaves, and had a beautiful blue rounded door on the front. The door had a little white round window at the top with four panes. There were many windows that went up the tree and throughout the limbs, and

some of the windows had flower boxes full of beautiful flowers attached. Oscar stepped closer, and reached out slowly and opened the blue door. The door made just a faint creaking sound as it opened, and Oscar was even more astonished by what was inside.

There were candles lit throughout his home, and it was fully furnished with a sofa, cushiony chairs, tables, a fireplace, and it smelled so good inside, like fresh linen! The fireplace was made of stones that went all the way up to the third floor. There were paintings of his family on the walls, and all the windows facing the back of the tree were big and rounded so the sunshine could come in, and then he saw the spiral staircase!

He walked up the staircase to the next floor and it was a bedroom. There was the most comfortable bed made of wood that had cozy blankets and soft pillows, and there was

a nightstand. There was a big oval metal tub right in his bedroom attached to the wall for bathing. It had a well pump, and a little plug was in the bottom of the tub that let the water run right back out of the tree for when he was finished.

The staircase kept going up, and he followed it along to the next room, the kitchen. There was a big cauldron, lots of hanging pots, and there were plates in the cupboards, utensils in the drawers, and a sink with a well pump that pumped fresh water to him straight from the stream that ran in front of his home. There were many more rooms upstairs that ran up the branches that were all furnished and his to do with as he pleased; many had fireplaces in them. At the very top of the tree was a bedroom that had a balcony so he could see over the entire forest. The balcony was furnished with rocking chairs, a table, and a swing so he could enjoy the view comfortably!

Oscar ran back down to the kitchen because he was very hungry, and he remembered the things his father told him about the tree. When he got into the kitchen, he sat at the table and thought to himself how delicious a roasted chicken with roasted vegetables would be, and suddenly, he smelled exactly what he had thought about! He got up and followed the smell to the oven next to the sink, pulled down on the oven door, and there it was, a piping hot dish of roasted chicken with gravy and vegetables. When he turned around to place the dish on the table, he noticed that the table was already set with his plate, a fork, a knife, fresh bread, and a glass of ice cold snonkelberry juice. He could not believe it! He sat down at the table and ate and ate until every morsel of food was gone and his belly was plump. Then he drank snonkelberry juice and bounced around on his bottom laughing for quite a while, and then went down to his bedroom and ran a nice warm bath for himself.

As he bathed, he stared at his bed anticipating the moment that he would crawl in it and snuggle with those fluffy pillows and warm blankets, for he had been sleeping on the ground and staying warm with shrubbery for too long! When his bath was finished, he pulled the plug and was amazed at how the water just ran down the side of the tree; he had never seen anything like it before! He then climbed into his soft bed, thought about his family back home in Norway and how much he missed them, and fell fast asleep.

The next morning, Oscar woke up and again was extremely excited about his new home. After he yawned, stretched, and looked around his bedroom a bit, he crawled out of bed and went to the kitchen and got a cup of hot tea and then headed outside to see the light of day. Just then, he heard Elle yelling "Oscar daring, where are you?" so Oscar put his tea down and ran to Elle in the flowery pasture.

He told her he had something exciting to tell her, but she had to promise that she would never say a word to anyone; Elle did promise. He told her about the seed that his father gave him, and told her of the tree, but he said that he could not tell her exactly where it was, but that he would always be able to hear her calling while he was in the Flowery Forest. Elle was incredibly happy that Oscar had his own home and was even happier knowing that he would be living close to her now permanently.

Oscar asked Elle "if you could have anything to eat in the world, what would it be"? Elle replied "Darling, I think if I could eat anything in the world that I wanted; it would have to be scrumptious toad stew"! "Toad stew, yuck!" he replied. Elle said, "I am a goblin darling, we like what we like!" Oscar told Elle to wait and that he would be right back.

Oscar ran up to his kitchen and sat down in the chair and thought about toad stew, and just then, he smelled the most awful smell coming from the oven, so he opened the oven and sure enough, there sat a piping hot pot of toad stew; it looked so disgusting to him! He saw frog legs and vegetables floating about in a dark green slimy sauce; it actually made him gag a bit. He quickly put a lid on the pot, grabbed a big spoon, grabbed some bread, and ran back to the pasture to present Elle with her favorite meal. Elle was in shock! She put both of her hands on either side of her face and exclaimed "Oscar, you didn't, how did you ever, Oh my!" She scooped up a big spoonful, tasted it and said, "Oh Oscar, this stew is the most extraordinary, divine thing I've ever tasted; Thank You"! She enjoyed the pot of stew, and then sopped up all the slimy sauce with the fresh bread, and then they headed down to the stream for a drink of water.

While sitting by the stream, Oscar explained to Elle how the tree works and told her that she too can have anything to eat that she wishes if she just asks him. He explained to her that she would never be able to see the tree because it only presents itself to him so that he may always stay safe. He told her that he may disappear occasionally but assured her that he would always return, so she need not worry. The two friends spent the day together laughing and frolicking about, and then Elle went home.

When Oscar returned to his tree, he walked in, brushed off his feet, and sat on his sofa to relax, but something shiny caught the corner of his eye on the sofa table. He got up to see what it was and saw a ring that was remarkably like the one on his thumb and a rolled-up scroll of paper that had instructions on it.

As he read the paper of instructions, it told him how he could go to any place in the world that he wished just by thinking of the location, and twisting the ring on his thumb around three times to the right, and that he would be able to return right back to his own parlor doing the same, but with three turns to the left. This was absolutely amazing, he thought to himself, this meant that he could travel the world if he liked, and most importantly, he could go back to visit his family that he missed so much! He was confused about the new ring that was like the one on his thumb, so he continued reading. At the bottom of the page of instructions, it stated that if he wanted to travel with someone, he could place the second ring on their thumb, and they could travel with him too but only if he held their hand during the journey; it also told him that the second ring could be seen by all.

Oscar decided to give it a try but before he did, he ran up to the kitchen and got a bottle of snonkelberry juice to take with him!

Chapter 5

Oscar Makes it Back Home

Oscar ran back down to his parlor, sat down on his sofa placing the second ring in his pocket, closed his eyes, and thought about being home with his father and mother. Then, in the midst of the thought, he twisted the ring on his thumb three times to the right, and when he opened his eyes, he was sitting in his childhood home in Norway, right in his parents parlor on the sofa, and his father was standing right in front of him. He jumped up and yelled "father, father, oh how I have missed you"! His father Clarence grabbed him and hugged him so tight and said, "I was wondering how long it would take you to get back home; welcome home son!" His mother Billi heard the commotion and was crying with joy at his return and decided that they must have a feast! It was a bit chilly in Norway, so they lit

the fireplace, and his mother prepared his favorite meal; farikal: mutton stew with cabbage and potatoes.

While the food was in the pot bubbling away and making the house smell delicious, the three of them sat in the parlor and talked about everything that had been going on in their lives. Oscar told his parents about his new friend Elle, and how they met, and about the journeys they went on, and he told them about how great and amazing his tree is! He then pulled out the bottle of snonkelberry juice and poured them both a glass. They were astonished at how the juice separated its colors with purple on the bottom, and green on top, and they carried on and on about it for they had never seen such a drink do that, but Oscar was waiting for them to take a drink!

His mother and father clanged their glasses together and then took a drink at the same time, and Oscar watched them both with a rascally grin on his face as they both began to turn purple. They were startled a bit with confusion while looking at each other's faces changing color, and then suddenly, they both began bouncing about on their bottoms in a circle laughing uncontrollably! When they stopped bouncing, their color returned and they were amazed at what a wonderful drink it was, and, still laughing, thanked Oscar.

After they ate the scrumptious dinner his mother made, they drank more snonkelberry juice and talked. Oscar told them that he had planned to see more of the world since he could travel so freely with his magical ring and told his father of the extra ring the tree had given him. He told his father how the ring worked and asked him to come back to England with him to see his home and meet his new friend Elle.

His father gladly accepted. So, Oscar put the ring on his father's thumb, he thought about his magical tree, twisted the ring three times to the left while holding his father's hand, and in the next blink of their eyes, they were right back in Oscars living parlor in England.

Oscar showed his father the whole tree, what it could do, and the comforts it provided, and then took him up to the top bedroom and told him to rest there so they could have a wonderful next day together. The next morning, Oscar ran upstairs and woke his father up, and he took him to the balcony to show him the beautiful view. As they looked over the green mountain scenery, they could see the trees shaking one by one as it seemed that something was coming closer to them, "it must be Elle, I can't wait for you to meet her father" says Oscar. Oscar and Clarence went to the kitchen, got some hot tea, lemony crumpets with creamy butter, grabbed a blanket, and ran down to the flowery pasture, and just as they arrived, they could hear Elle "Oscar darling, are you there?" "Top of the morning to you my dear Elle, there is someone I would love for you to meet; my father Clarence" said Oscar, "Your father, oh it is so very nice to meet you Clarence, Oscar has told me much about you darling" replied Elle. Clarence was in awe at how big Elle was and was startled a bit by her size and look but said "It is an honor to meet you as well Miss Elle, Oscar has told me much about you too." The three of them then sat down on the blanket and enjoyed their breakfast while talking. Clarence asked Elle where she lived, and she informed him and Oscar that she lives in a cave not far away, and her parents and two brothers live close to her. She said that she would love to take them and show them her home, but she was scared that her brothers would smell them, and that if they did, it would put them in danger. Clarence said that he would love to see where, and how she lived anyway.

Chapter 6

A Close Call

Elle decided that she could probably sneak them into her cave to show them, and then sneak them back out safely, so she put Oscar on her shoulder, and she placed Clarence in a pocket in her dress, and off they went. Clarence had never had such a ride like this; it was a very bouncy one! Elle ran quickly through the forest, and just before she got to her cave, she stopped and stood behind a big tree, and slowly peeked out to see if any of her family was out, and just as she thought, no one was up yet. So, she tip-toed right into her cave, and closed her cave door so they would not be bothered. Elle's cave had a big sofa, a big chair, a big bed, big tables, and everything was so big to Oscar and Clarence, it was also lit up with big candles, and had a very strange, stinky smell; a smell they had never smelled before.

They all three sat in Elle's home talking about things while sipping tea, and suddenly, there was a loud bang on Elle's cave door. The bang was so loud and hard that it bounced Oscar and Clarence right out of the big chair they were sitting on. Elle went to the door and cracked it just a bit, just to see one of her brothers standing there. Oscar and Clarence were scared to see such a great big goblin, much taller, and way bigger than Elle, with a huge nose, and just three strands of hair standing up right in the middle of his head. Elle said, "Good morning, Wilbur, what can I do for you darling?" Wilbur told Elle that he had left his socks there, and needed to retrieve them so he could wear them that day. Elle told Wilbur that she would find them, but he had to wait outside. Elle left the door cracked and began walking around looking for Wilbur's socks; all the while, Oscar and Clarence were hiding behind the huge chair that they fell out of, watching every move that Wilbur made. As Elle walked around searching for the socks, the two trolls noticed that Wilbur had stuck his nose in the air and began sniffing, his head moving back and forth with every sniff. He then decided to peek his head in the cave door to further smell the curious scent. Elle finally saw the socks lying by her fireplace, scooped them up, and headed for the door. The trolls saw the socks as she grabbed them, and noticed that a dark, thick, slimy sludge was dripping from them. Then, as she passed the trolls with the socks, a gust of green stink hit them right in the face! They both turned green for a moment and gagged a bit, but finally caught their breath again, and they were relieved that the socks were gone. They then knew what that strange stinky smell was that they first

smelled when they entered the cave, and never wanted to smell that stench again!

Elle handed Wilbur his socks, and then Wilbur said to Elle in a very deep, dopey voice, "Elle, hu uh hu, you have something in here that smells delicious" Elle said "I have no such thing, and I'm surprised that you can smell anything other than those stinky socks, now go home!" Wilbur replied, "Uh, yea, huh, I smell something good, I'm gonna see what it is." Wilbur began coming into the cave, and Elle immediately snatched his stinky, slimy, sludgy socks out of his hand, and hit him right in his big nose with them. Wilbur's nose bounced up and down and side to side and made a loud, funny sound. He grabbed his nose so it would stop bouncing, and then he yelled at Elle to stop, and she yelled at him to get out, pushing him back out the cave door as she yelled, and then threw the socks at him and slammed the door; Wilbur did leave holding his nose, and did not come back that day! Elle looked at Oscar and Clarence and said, "that was a close one darling, I had better get you two back before the others show up!"

Elle placed both Oscar and Clarence in her pocket, sneaked back out of her cave, and ran back to the Flowery Forest safely with not one of her brothers noticing.

Oscar told Elle about his ring, and the second ring, and what they were capable of doing. Elle could not see the ring on his thumb because it was part of his tree, invisible to all but him. He told Elle that he had planned to travel, but he would be back soon and that he loved her company, for she was his best friend. Elle's eyes lit up, and she said that she was eager to hear the stories that he would bring back and was excited for him.

Oscar, Clarence, and Elle walked about the forest all day enjoying each other's company with delightful stories and lots of laughs, and then the day drew long, and Elle had to go home. Oscar and Clarence were also tired, so they went back to the magical tree. Oscar and his father had a wonderful meal of sausages with onion gravy and mashed potatoes, and then each took a hot bath, and climbed into bed for the night.

Chapter 7

Bringing Billi to England

The next morning, Clarence woke Oscar up and told him that they really should go back to Norway and have a home cooked Norwegian breakfast made by his mother, because they both knew that Billi missed them, and they missed her. Oscar agreed, and placed the ring on his father's thumb and held his hand, thought about his home back in Norway, and with three twists to the right; they were back at Oscar's childhood home, right in the parlor. They both ran upstairs and woke Oscar's mother up and she was extremely glad to see them. She put on her robe and slippers and went downstairs and made a wonderful Norwegian breakfast: open faced sandwiches made with fresh bread, and topped with creamy butter, smoked fish, and cheese, and three glasses of snonkelberry juice; one for each of them.

Oscar and his parents spent the morning talking, and Oscar told his parents that he wanted them both to come back to England with him. He said that all he needs to do is take one at a time and told them that anytime they wanted to return home to Norway, he would return them one by one as well. They both agreed, gathered some things, and off they went with three twists to the left of the ring. His mother Billi was astonished by the tree and incredibly happy to be there.

After Oscar showed his mother around and told her all about Elle, they sat in the kitchen and had the most delightful meal that she had ever had. During lunch, Oscar asked his father how he came about getting the seed. Clarence told him that his grandfather Leon had given it to him, and his grandfather also told him of great tales that he had in Ireland with the leprechauns. Clarence said that he was told that Leon got the seed from an old man that lived deep in a forest in Ireland. Oscar decided that he really wanted to see this place that his grandfather Leon had described, so he and Clarence decided that they would make a trip soon.

After lunch, all three went to the flowery pasture because they heard Elle coming and Oscar wanted his mother to meet her. Billi and Elle hit it right off and giggled and laughed at the stories each one told about their lives and of Oscar. Oscar told Elle that he and his father had planned to make a trip to Ireland and asked her if she would keep his mother company while they were away, and she gladly agreed. After Elle went home, the three walked back to the tree and they marked the path with stones so Billi would have no trouble finding her way back while they were gone, since she did not have her own ring to wear and could not see the tree from the outside.

The next day, Oscar and his parents got up and had a wonderful breakfast together. He and his father decided that just before nightfall, they would head to Ireland, and they did just that. As they sat in the parlor of the tree, they held each other's hand as Billi watched, and then they thought about Ireland and the leprechauns, and with three twists of the ring to the right, they opened their eyes, and they were there!

Chapter 8

The Rainbow Forest

Oscar and Clarence were amazed at how beautiful it was there. The land was very green as far as their eyes could see, and it had rolling hills. And, as they looked up, they noticed that the trees were the colors of the rainbow, and that each tree had different bright colored leaves, and there were many different shaped leaves on every tree; so, they knew that they must be close to the leprechauns. They walked together through the Rainbow Forest for a while admiring the beautiful trees as they were blowing back and forth, and when night finally arrived, they stumbled upon a village down in a valley.

Oscar and Clarence hid at the edge of the forest above the village and just watched.

They saw lots of green grass roof cottages with smoke coming out of the chimneys, animals running around, they heard laughing and talking, and then something very scrumptious smelling began to fill the air as the wind blew towards them, and beautiful music began playing. They heard flutes, drums, fiddles, harps, and other kinds of instruments they could not quite make out. They decided to get a better look at what was going on, so they walked to where they could see the other side of the village while still staying on the edge of the forest. When they got to the other side, they saw a bonfire and many leprechauns dancing about in the village; this looked like the place they wanted to be for the night, but they were not sure how welcome they would be!

They decided that they would take a chance and go into the village, so they walked down the hill, and sneaked through the big rainbow gate.

They tip-toed through the shadows and found a wagon that was close to the bonfire, and they ran and hid underneath it while watching the little leprechauns sing and dance. They noticed there was something roasting above the fire, and that each leprechaun would take turns turning the handle, so the food cooked on all sides. Whatever it was, it smelled delicious to Oscar and Clarence, for the trip had made them very hungry!

They hid awhile under the wagon watching all that was going on, and then they saw one leprechaun walk over and sprinkle spices on the roasting food; just then, a gust of wind blew and took the spice with it right to the nose of Clarence! Clarence's nose began to tickle, and he began to sniffle, and his face started turning red. Oscar looked at Clarence and knew that he was on the verge of sneezing, and then Clarence began making a quietly-loud sound of "ah, ah"; Oscar then quickly grabbed Clarence's nose and pinched it until Clarence's need to sneeze threat seemed to be gone, and then let go. But as soon as Oscar let go, Clarence let out a great big loud "AWW CHOO, AWW CHOO, AWW CHOO"! As soon as Clarence sneezed, the music stopped, the dancing stopped, and all the leprechauns were peering right at them! They both were frozen for a moment, and then slowly eased from beneath the wagon. As they stood up off the ground, they brushed off all the dust, grass, and clovers that were stuck to their clothes. Then, leprechaun guards quickly surrounded them and pointed their long, bright, colorful poles, that had sharp arrows on the tips at them. And suddenly, the largest leprechaun, who was also wearing a crown, ran over to them and said in a very Irish voice "now, what do we have here"! Oscar and Clarence introduced themselves, and Oscar told the big leprechaun where they were from and what brought them to the village; the stories that came from their grandfather Leon. The leprechaun king was a bit uneasy with his story at first but then asked them "was your grandfather Leon a Norwegian man"? They both exclaimed at the same time "YES"! He then asked them "was this Leon from Tønsberg?" and they both happily replied "YES"! The leprechaun king then ordered the guards to stand down and ordered the feast to be served! He said to Oscar and Clarence while chuckling "Yes, yes, Leon and I had some great adventures back in the day! Tell me, what ever became of ole Leon, I haven't heard from him in ages"? Oscar looked at Clarence very inquisitive himself waiting for the answer, and Clarence said, "my grandfather went on an excursion with a fleet of ships looking for new land, and there was a big storm, and, he was never heard from again; none of the ships were found, and it's been years". The king shook his head in disbelief and told them both how sorry he was to hear that. He then began walking, and Oscar and Clarence followed towards the feast hall as he said, "Leon was an exceptional troll" and proceeded with "Well, I am King Wallace, and you both are welcome here at Rainbow Village for as long as you like. We will feast and get to know each other, and then I will set you both up with a cottage to rest for the night or however long you wish to stay, you are my guests"! Oscar and Clarence were very relieved and happy to have met new friends, and a friend of Leon's!

They sat at the table both on either side of the king and the food began to come out. The leprechauns were bringing out dish after dish, placing one dish at a time on each of the big, round tables while singing songs and dancing about, and pouring rainbow juice into all the goblets that were on the tables. When all the

food was out, the king stood up, and everyone else followed suit. He held up his goblet and said, "I wish to make a toast to our new friends, grandsons of Leon" and all the leprechauns held up their goblets and shouted "Slainte"! They all then feasted on roasted mutton, sausages, cabbage, potatoes, desserts and much more until they were happy and plump.

After they were done with the feast, they all sat around the bonfire and King Wallace told them delightful stories about their grandfather Leon. One story he told Oscar and Clarence was about He and Leon and the Snobblehobs. Oscar and Clarence had never heard of a Snobblehob before, so King Wallace told them all about them. He said that the Snobblehobs are a group of creatures that live just over two mountains away from the Rainbow Village just on the outskirts of the Rainbow Forest. He described them as a scary looking bunch and told them that they are very mean, big but not smart, and they love to eat small critters. He told them that he and Leon were captured by the Snobblehobs and locked away in a dungeon many years ago. His story went on to tell that Leon was able to slip through the jail bars, but just barely because he was a small troll, and Leon eased the key right out of the sleeping Snobblehob guard's hand. He then, slowly, and quietly unlocked the door, and they both tip-toed out of the dungeon. When they got out of the dungeon, the guard had woken up and noticed that they were gone and blew a very loud horn. It was then that all the Snobblehobs were on alert and began searching for them. He said that he and Leon saw a tree and ran to the very top of it, and while sitting on a branch, they watched all the Snobblehobs below as they ran around looking in and under things while all bumping into one another and falling down; they were trying not to make any noise as they quietly giggled at how silly the Snobblehobs were. After some time, the Snobblehobs began giving up on the search and began going into their huts for the night. He said there were a few left searching and he and Leon felt that they had a good chance to escape, so they both eased down the tree quietly to the last branch. After sitting on the branch for a while longer, the Snobblehobs that were still looking headed toward their direction, and it was then that they made their break. Leon jumped down on one of the Snobblehobs head, and then he jumped onto a Snobblehobs head, and they both continued to bounce from Snobblehob head to Snobblehob head on each Snobblehob until they got close to the gate. Then they jumped onto the ground, raced out the gate, ran straight into the Rainbow Forest, and ran until they were far away from danger.

King Wallace, Oscar, and Clarence laughed and laughed envisioning the story, and then decided to head in for the night.

Oscar and Clarence stayed some time there with King Wallace in the Rainbow Village; making a trip back to their own magical tree a couple of times to check on Billi and Elle, and during their visit they told the king about the seed that Leon had given them. Clarence told the king that Leon mentioned that he got it from an old man in Ireland, and they wanted to know if he knew anything about this old man. The king told them both that he knew that Leon had visited a wise old man with two daughters that lived about two days away from them deep in the Sugar Mill Forest. He warned them that to get to this forest, they would have to pass through the Nob Forest, and past the Snobblehob village.

Chapter 9

The Nob Forest

The two trolls wanted an adventure and wanted to see the land of Ireland, so they chose to walk instead of using their rings. So, they packed some food, drinks, and their belongings and headed out into the Rainbow Forest. They walked and walked until daylight began to fade, found a nice little flowery pasture on top of a hill, and decided to camp there until the morning. From the top of the hill, they could see the Rainbow Forest's colors fading into a darker forest not far in the distance; they knew they were getting close to the Nob Forest, so they built a fire, ate, and settled in for the night. They had bread, mutton, and berries and then they laid down and fell asleep after talking and laughing for a good while.

Suddenly, in the middle of the night, Clarence felt a stick poking him in the belly. He opened his eyes slowly as he yawned and stretched thinking it was Oscar, and then he screamed! The scream woke Oscar up, and then he screamed; they were surrounded by a group of big scary creatures standing over and peering down on them both! The creatures had big round faces, big noses, and pointy ears. They were covered with short reddish-brown hair, had long arms, stood upright on two short legs, and had very plump bellies and yellow eyes. They then heard one of the creatures say in a deep slow voice "critters for Snobblehobs" and the others cheered as they scooped up Oscar and Clarence and threw them in a big bag.

As they grabbed Clarence, his ring fell off onto the ground and a Snobblehob saw it and picked it up. Oscar said to Clarence "father, hurry and give me your hand"

and Clarence replied "my ring slipped off my thumb when I was grabbed Oscar;" they both looked at each other and knew that they had gotten themselves into a big mess!

The two trolls bumbled around in the bag for a bit as they listened to the Snobblehobs feet march loudly, and then they felt the bag being tossed down hard. Oscar and Clarence bounced off the floor, and Oscar's foot hit Clarence right in the head, "ouch son" said Clarence as he held his head. Suddenly, the bag opened, and they both looked up and saw a big hand reach into the bag that pulled them out one by one, rolling them both in a dungeon cell as if they were bowling balls. They felt doomed as they watched and heard the cell door slam but were relieved to see the Snobblehob walk away.

They noticed that the dungeon was dimly lit with flickering candles hanging on the walls, and they saw a big chair sitting right outside their cell and a big table across the hall with another chair next to it. As they walked around the damp, musky-smelling cell, they saw many names etched into the rock walls. They stumbled across one etching that said Leon and KW; they knew at once who those names belonged to! One of the Snobblehob guards came in and sat down in the big chair by the table, and Oscar and Clarence scooched back into a dark corner and sat there for hours trying to figure a way out. After more time passed, another Snobblehob guard walked in and handed a small, shiny, silver ring to the sitting guard, and then slowly said, "we found this when we caught them two critters right there" and pointed over to the two trolls. The sitting guard took the ring and sat it on the table, and then slowly yelled "get out and leave me be, you've uh, ruined my tryin' ta get ta sleep!" so the other guard quickly shuffled out.

Oscar and Clarence knew that they had to get that ring quick before they became Snobblehob dinner and were eager for that guard to go to sleep! They both stayed back in the corner of the cell, hiding in the dark nervously and quietly, until the guard began snoring. Oscar then tip-toed to the cell door, and slipped through the bars easily, and then tip-toed ever so quietly to the table and eased the big stick out from between the guard's fingers. He then knocked the ring on the floor with the stick, and it made a loud "ting" sound when it hit, and the guard began to move around restlessly. Just as Oscar bent down and picked up the ring, the guard woke and stood yelling slowly "hey you, you-you wait right there and give me back that ring!" as he was standing right in between Oscar and the cell door. Oscar, holding the ring tightly, ran right between the Snobblehobs legs, slipped back through the bars of the cell door, and ran over to his father. All the while, the guard was fumbling around with the keys trying to get the cell door open; just as he did, Clarence got the ring back on his thumb, and Oscar and Clarence held each other's hands while thinking of the Sugar Mill Forest. They twisted the ring three times to the right, and suddenly disappeared right into thin air; just as the Snobblehob guards two arms reached out to swoop them up! When Oscar and Clarence opened their eyes, they were running into the Sugar Mill Forest safe and far away from all the Snobblehobs and all danger. They looked at each other with beads of sweat pouring down their foreheads and gave each other a big hug; for they knew that was a close call!

Chapter 10

The Sugar Mill Forest

Daylight had just appeared in the Sugar Mill Forest when Oscar and Clarence arrived, and as they looked around, they saw that the ground was lush green and moist with fresh dew. They also noticed that there were little milky white crystals lying randomly all over the ground that gleamed when the sunlight hit them, and that there was a sweet smell that blew in the wind. They saw that the trees were big and green, and that each tree produced different types of fruits, berries, and sweets, so every time the trees blew, they let off the scent of their delicious harvest. The two trolls heard the trickle of water, and they saw many beautiful animals wandering about peacefully. They were extremely excited and relieved to be in this forest safe, and comfortable,

and they knew that they were one step closer to finding out the origin of Oscar's tree.

They decided to walk, so they followed the trickle sound until they reached a brook. They were very thirsty so they both kneeled down and reached their cupped hands in the crystal-clear blue water and drank and drank. Clarence said to Oscar "have you ever had such sweet water before Oscar?" and Oscar replied "no, and it's so delicious." After they quenched their thirst, they chose to follow the path of the brook and see where it took them. As they walked, they saw animals along the bank drinking, and they saw lots of fish jumping out and back into the water, and beautiful, colorful birds flew everywhere as they chirped and sang their songs. They walked up and down many hills for quite a while, and then came to a little wooden bridge that sat at the foot of a waterfall. The bridge

was narrow but high, and was wet with the mist from the waterfall, and the other end continued to go on through a tree tunnel.

Oscar and Clarence took the bridge route and ended up on a path that was paved with stones. The stones sparkled and shined and led them all the way up to the top of a hill where a cottage sat. As they were getting closer to the cottage, they heard the voices of two ladies, so they stopped, slipped behind a big tree, and just watched for a bit. They saw that each of the ladies was holding a bag, and they were both picking things off the ground. Both ladies were short, but much taller than both Oscar and Clarence; one had short light hair and the other had short dark hair. They each had big brown eyes and wore long dresses that came past the knees; one lady's dress was purple and orange, and the other lady's dress was pink and orange;

and both wore big orange hats. They both wore socks halfway up to their knees with boots, and each walked wobbling side to side. The ladies just kept talking and talking over each other, and it seemed that neither one was listening to the other, then they would both start laughing at the same time. This was very odd to the two trolls, but they kept watching and listening although they could not understand anything the ladies were saying.

After the old ladies had collected enough of whatever it was that they were collecting, they wobbled uphill towards the cottage and just disappeared right into thin air. Oscar and Clarence were very curious now; they wanted to know how the two disappeared so suddenly. The trolls got back on the path, walked up to the cottage, and rang a bell that hung right outside the door. They heard some scuffling,

and a voice that yelled "coming" and then they saw an old man open the door "Yes, how might I help you two gentlemen today?" said the old man. Oscar replied, "I am Oscar, and this is my father Clarence, and we came today because King Wallace told us that you may have known our grandfather Leon, and that you may know about the magical seed that he gave us." Then the old man replied, "Oh my, that was many, many, years ago, but yes, Leon was a great friend of mine, please, do come in." Oscar and Clarence entered the cottage, and the old man offered them a seat, so they sat on a lovely little sofa in front of a warm fire.

The old man was short and looked frail as he scampered slowly with a cane. He wore brown trousers with front pockets, a white shirt tucked in, black suspenders, a green tartan cap, and a green tartan coat. He had dark shoes with striped socks, and he had a very round face with pink cheeks, a big round nose, and green eyes. He had a snow-white beard, mustache, and hair, and of course he was wearing a red bow tie; he looked very distinguished! He said, "I am Sir Jude, I am honored to have the family of my friend Leon in my home, it is very nice to meet you." He then told them as he poured them tea that his two daughters were cooking dinner and offered them both to stay and eat. The trolls gladly accepted and they all three sat in the cottage sipping tea while talking.

Clarence asked Sir Jude how he met Leon, and the old man laughed as he told them that he met Leon while traveling in Norway. He said that one night, two big trolls saw him as he was strolling around in downtown Tønsberg and began chasing him, and then suddenly, something made them both fall, and that after the ground stopped rumbling and the dust had settled, he saw Leon laughing while running towards him. He said Leon then grabbed his hand and led him into a door in the ground; they both then jumped into the hole and shut the door and waited until all was quiet outside and they knew the two big trolls were gone. He said that Leon saved his life that night, and they became great friends.

Just as he finished the story, the two ladies walked in the door. They were both talking non-stop at the same time about nothing that anyone could understand, with one holding a black cauldron of bubbling hot delicious-smelling mushroom stew, and the other one holding fresh bread and a blueberry pie. Sir Jude said, "These are my two daughters, Faye and Kaye," the trolls replied at the same time "It's very nice to meet you ladies" and the two ladies just giggled as they blushed with their heads down, and then began rambling on amongst themselves again. They all sat at a short round table and the sisters served up the food.

While eating dinner, Oscar and Clarence said that they watched as the sisters collected what they found out were mushrooms, and then saw them disappear into thin air, Sir Jude laughed. He informed them that the sisters live inside the hill, and that there is a tunnel in the ground that they jump in and slide down into their home, so they don't have to walk back down the hill and behind the waterfall to enter their front door; the trolls laughed and thought that was very clever.

After dinner, they all sat by the fire again, and Oscar and Clarence asked Sir Jude about the magical tree seed that Leon had given them. Then, the wise old man told them that he had given that seed to Leon for saving his life; he wanted Leon to always be safe, and he wanted Leon to be able to visit him in Ireland whenever he wanted to, so, he gave him the magical seed; he also let them know that he had given Leon more than one seed. Sir Jude then asked them why Leon had given them the seed. Clarence told him that his grandfather gave it to him just before he left to go on his journey, because he wanted him to always be safe. Clarence said that he always felt safe at his home in Norway, so he kept the seed because he knew that one day he would need it, and that day came when Oscar grew too little.

The two trolls then asked Sir Jude where he got the seeds and where they came from, and Sir Jude responded: "Many magical seeds were given to me and my father many years ago by a beggar that my father and I helped. I was a young man, and I was in the city of Rome helping my father with work. It was early evening, and my father and I had just left an INN after eating dinner, and as we were walking, we saw a man sitting on the ground asking for help. He was shaking because he was cold, and he looked thin, pale, and hungry, so we offered him the leftovers that we were taking back to our rented room, and he gladly accepted with the most amazing and tranquil smile. He looked broken from the outside, but his attitude and smile seemed as if he were a happy soul. He had torn and raggedy clothes, and scuffed up shoes, but also had a gleam in his eye that I had never seen before. The man's name was Livingston, and I shall never forget him. He ate the food so quickly and was still hungry, so my father and I went back to the INN and got another meal for him and came back and gave it to him. We sat with him for a while and talked with him as he ate the food, and then my father offered him his warm sweater, and as he was pulling it off, I heard a noise and looked

away, and when we both looked back at him, the man had just vanished. In the place where he sat were many seeds that sat on top of a note, and the note read:

"I sat here many a night just as I did tonight and was passed up by hundreds of people that never looked twice at me as I sat here hungry and cold. But you two gentlemen did stop, and out of the kindness of your heart, you helped a stranger. I leave with you these magical seeds that will ensure that you both always have a safe home, an adventurous life, and never go hungry; people like you deserve it; thank you! Each seed will grow into a big tree home, each a bit different than the next, and will only be visible from the outside to the ring bearer's; plant and gift them wisely. Livingston~."

Sir Jude walked over to the fireplace, opened a box on the mantle, and took out a folded parchment. He then handed it to Clarence and Oscar, and they were

I sat here many a night just as I did tonight and was passed up by hundreds of people that never looked twice at me as I sat here hungry and cold. But you two gentlemen did stop, and out of the kindness of your heart, you helped a stranger. I leave with you these magical seeds that will ensure that you both always have a safe home, an adventurous life, and never go hungry; people like you deserve it; thank you! Each seed will grow into a big tree home, each a bit different than the next, and will only be visible from the outside to the ring bearer's; plant and gift them wisely.

Livingston~

excited to read in it the words that Sir Jude had just spoken; it was the letter from Livingston. Sir Jude spoke again as he reached in the same box that the letter was in, and pulled something else out; "This is all I know, I have mine planted far away in another country, but I choose to live here in the Sugar Mill forest with my daughters, although, I still love to get away from time to time. I would like to give you another seed if I may, for you two are the only worthy ones that I have found in my many years, and the only ones that I have met who know about the magical seeds." He then handed Clarence the magical seed, and the two trolls thanked him with amazement on their faces. Oscar and Clarence told Sir Jude that they must leave soon to get back to their life in England with Billi and Elle, but asked if they could come back to visit him now and then, and he told them that they are welcome anytime to visit and thanked them for the wonderful company.

Oscar and Clarence wanted to see the waterfall again before they left, so, Sir Jude told Faye and Kaye to take them through the shortcut. The ladies mumbled and giggled as the trolls followed them out the door, and Sir Jude watched and waved goodbye as each one disappeared down the tunnel. Clarence and Oscar laughed loudly as they slid side to side quickly down the slippery slide, and they landed softly on a big cushion. They stood up, and Faye and Kaye showed them around their cozy home and then walked them to the front door.

Oscar and Clarence walked out the door onto a porch, heard the sound of raging water, and saw that they were right behind the waterfall. On either side of the waterfall, they saw a rainbow in the mist; it was unbelievably beautiful, and tranquil, and they thought that it would be a good place to say goodbye to

Ireland. After dipping their hands in the waterfall and taking a drink of the sweet water, they held each other's hand while thinking of their magical tree back in England, twisted the ring three times to the left, and off they went; when they opened their eyes, they were sitting in their own parlor in the Flowery Forest.

Chapter 11

Back Home in the Flowery Forest

It was midday when they returned home, and Billi was not home in the tree, so they ran out and called her name. They heard Elle's voice "Oscar and Clarence, we are over here darlings," so they followed her voice to the flowery pasture, and Elle and Billi gave them great big hugs and were happy they were back home. Billi ran back to the tree to get supper and brought it back along with a big bottle of snonkelberry juice, and they all sat on a blanket feasting, talking, laughing, and all but Elle, bouncing about on their bottoms.

Oscar and Clarence told them all about the leprechauns, King Wallace, the Snobblehobs, Sir Jude, the sisters, the story of Livingston, and the way everything looked, tasted, and smelled.

They said after dinner how glad they were to be back and decided that they would take a break from traveling for a while.

When they were all done eating and talking about the trip, they took a stroll through the Flowery Forest admiring all the birds, deer, rabbits, foxes, and other critters. And, as they watched the sun draw closer to the horizon, they enjoyed the lovely breeze that left a sweet scent in the air. Elle said that she must be getting home before night arrived, and the trolls agreed that they should all do the same.

Oscar and his parents headed back to the tree and stopped by the kitchen to get a pot of tea as they headed up to the balcony. When they reached the balcony, Billi poured each one a cup of tea, and then each took a rocking chair and watched the beauty of the day as it was disappearing. In the distance, they could see each tree shake one by one, and they knew

that it was Elle heading back home. As they rocked in the chairs, they saw colors of blue, orange, pink, and purple streaking through the sky as the sun was painting her final picture of the day, and they watched it fade away. They all agreed that their lives had turned out to be exceptionally wonderful because of the selfless act of their grandfather Leon, and discussed how they would have never met Elle or had the opportunity to experience the things that they had so far if it were not for him.

After the sun had no more light to shine for the day, they went into their magical tree and turned in for bed. They hugged each other and expressed their love, and each snuggled in the warm, cozy beds that the tree had given them. As Oscar listened, he could hear the hoot of an owl, crickets chirping, and the trickle of the stream. And as he rolled over, he smiled big and closed his eyes, for he knew that tomorrow would be another grand day, and he was happy that it was on its way!

The End